# WHAT'S WRONG
## AT THE
# BEACH?

## ILLUSTRATED BY JOHN HOLLADAY

There are five things wrong
in each colorful scene.
Can you find them all?

SMITHMARK

BEACH COOKOUT

THE BOARDWALK

# THE MARINA

A SAND CASTLE CONTEST

# THE TIDE POOL

SNORKELING

PLAYING VOLLEYBALL

# ANSWERS

There are five things wrong in each scene.

**BEACH COOKOUT** (1) snow on tree; (2) man carrying toboggan; (3) man with flowerpot on head; (4) woman wearing nightgown and slippers; (5) water-skier pulling boat.

**THE BOARDWALK** (1) huge banana split; (2) apple on post; (3) backwards car on Ferris wheel; (4) man carrying Christmas tree; (5) orange instead of umbrella.

**THE MARINA** (1) dog on roller skates; (2) striped pole; (3) woman wearing winter gloves; (4) bird wearing shoes; (5) huge present behind building.

**THE PIER** (1) man not sitting in boat; (2) telephone instead of fishing line; (3) fisherman carrying baseball bat; (4) upside-down lamp in window; (5) strange bird under pier.